Business Name:

_____

_____

_____

Financial Year:

_____

_____

_____

About the Author

This simple cash book has been created by Jane E Kelly who is the author of several books, including Bookkeeping for Dummies, Sage 50 Accounts for Dummies and more recently has compiled and co-authored Bookkeeping & Accounting All In One for Dummies (all Wiley Publications).

Jane realised that there is a need for micro businesses or those just starting out, to document their business transactions in a simple way. This book is great for those who hate spreadsheets but love journals!

Copyright

INCOME/EXPENSE LEDGER

Month:	Year:

Date	Description	Income	Expense	Balance
	Opening balance / Balance b/fwd	*		
	Closing balance / Balance c/fwd	*		

* Delete as appropriate

If you need more space, carry your balance forward to the next page.
If you have reached the end of your month/period, then check that the Closing balance
above, agrees to your Bank Statement for the same period.
Use a fresh page for each new month.

INCOME/EXPENSE LEDGER

Month:			Year:		

Date	Description	Income	Expense	Balance
	Opening balance / Balance b/fwd	*		
	Closing balance / Balance c/fwd	*		

* Delete as appropriate

If you need more space, carry your balance forward to the next page.
If you have reached the end of your month/period, then check that the Closing balance
above, agrees to your Bank Statement for the same period.
Use a fresh page for each new month.

INCOME/EXPENSE LEDGER

Month:				Year:

Date	Description	Income	Expense	Balance
	Opening balance / Balance b/fwd *			
	Closing balance / Balance c/fwd *			

* Delete as appropriate

If you need more space, carry your balance forward to the next page.
If you have reached the end of your month/period, then check that the Closing balance above, agrees to your Bank Statement for the same period.
Use a fresh page for each new month.

INCOME/EXPENSE LEDGER

Month:			Year:		

Date	Description	Income	Expense	Balance
	Opening balance / Balance b/fwd *			
	Closing balance / Balance c/fwd *			

* Delete as appropriate

If you need more space, carry your balance forward to the next page.
If you have reached the end of your month/period, then check that the Closing balance above, agrees to your Bank Statement for the same period.
Use a fresh page for each new month.

INCOME/EXPENSE LEDGER

Month:			Year:	

Date	Description	Income	Expense	Balance
	Opening balance / Balance b/fwd *			
	Closing balance / Balance c/fwd *			

* Delete as appropriate

If you need more space, carry your balance forward to the next page.
If you have reached the end of your month/period, then check that the Closing balance above, agrees to your Bank Statement for the same period.
Use a fresh page for each new month.

INCOME/EXPENSE LEDGER

Month: **Year:**

Date	Description	Income	Expense	Balance
	Opening balance / Balance b/fwd	*		
	Closing balance / Balance c/fwd	*		

* Delete as appropriate

If you need more space, carry your balance forward to the next page.
If you have reached the end of your month/period, then check that the Closing balance above, agrees to your Bank Statement for the same period.
Use a fresh page for each new month.

INCOME/EXPENSE LEDGER

Month: **Year:**

Date	Description	Income	Expense	Balance
	Opening balance / Balance b/fwd *			
	Closing balance / Balance c/fwd *			

* Delete as appropriate

If you need more space, carry your balance forward to the next page.
If you have reached the end of your month/period, then check that the Closing balance above, agrees to your Bank Statement for the same period.
Use a fresh page for each new month.

INCOME/EXPENSE LEDGER

Month:			Year:	

Date	Description	Income	Expense	Balance
	Opening balance / Balance b/fwd	*		
	Closing balance / Balance c/fwd	*		

* Delete as appropriate

If you need more space, carry your balance forward to the next page.
If you have reached the end of your month/period, then check that the Closing balance above, agrees to your Bank Statement for the same period.
Use a fresh page for each new month.

INCOME/EXPENSE LEDGER

Month: **Year:**

Date	Description	Income	Expense	Balance
	Opening balance / Balance b/fwd	*		
	Closing balance / Balance c/fwd	*		

* Delete as appropriate

If you need more space, carry your balance forward to the next page.
If you have reached the end of your month/period, then check that the Closing balance
above, agrees to your Bank Statement for the same period.
Use a fresh page for each new month.

INCOME/EXPENSE LEDGER

Month:			Year:	

Date	Description	Income	Expense	Balance
	Opening balance / Balance b/fwd *			
	Closing balance / Balance c/fwd *			

* Delete as appropriate

If you need more space, carry your balance forward to the next page.
If you have reached the end of your month/period, then check that the Closing balance above, agrees to your Bank Statement for the same period.
Use a fresh page for each new month.

INCOME/EXPENSE LEDGER

Month:	Year:

Date	Description	Income	Expense	Balance
	Opening balance / Balance b/fwd	*		
	Closing balance / Balance c/fwd	*		

* Delete as appropriate

If you need more space, carry your balance forward to the next page.
If you have reached the end of your month/period, then check that the Closing balance
above, agrees to your Bank Statement for the same period.
Use a fresh page for each new month.

INCOME/EXPENSE LEDGER

Month:	Year:

Date	Description	Income	Expense	Balance
	Opening balance / Balance b/fwd	*		
	Closing balance / Balance c/fwd	*		

* Delete as appropriate

If you need more space, carry your balance forward to the next page.
If you have reached the end of your month/period, then check that the Closing balance above, agrees to your Bank Statement for the same period.
Use a fresh page for each new month.

INCOME/EXPENSE LEDGER

Month:		Year:		

Date	Description	Income	Expense	Balance
	Opening balance / Balance b/fwd	*		
	Closing balance / Balance c/fwd	*		

* Delete as appropriate

If you need more space, carry your balance forward to the next page.
If you have reached the end of your month/period, then check that the Closing balance above, agrees to your Bank Statement for the same period.
Use a fresh page for each new month.

INCOME/EXPENSE LEDGER

Month:	Year:

Date	Description	Income	Expense	Balance
	Opening balance / Balance b/fwd	*		
	Closing balance / Balance c/fwd	*		

* Delete as appropriate

If you need more space, carry your balance forward to the next page.
If you have reached the end of your month/period, then check that the Closing balance
above, agrees to your Bank Statement for the same period.
Use a fresh page for each new month.

INCOME/EXPENSE LEDGER

Month: **Year:**

Date	Description	Income	Expense	Balance
	Opening balance / Balance b/fwd	*		
	Closing balance / Balance c/fwd	*		

* Delete as appropriate

If you need more space, carry your balance forward to the next page.
If you have reached the end of your month/period, then check that the Closing balance above, agrees to your Bank Statement for the same period.
Use a fresh page for each new month.

INCOME/EXPENSE LEDGER

| Month: | | | Year: | |

Date	Description	Income	Expense	Balance
	Opening balance / Balance b/fwd	*		
	Closing balance / Balance c/fwd	*		

* Delete as appropriate

If you need more space, carry your balance forward to the next page.
If you have reached the end of your month/period, then check that the Closing balance
above, agrees to your Bank Statement for the same period.
Use a fresh page for each new month.

INCOME/EXPENSE LEDGER

Month:				Year:

Date	Description	Income	Expense	Balance
	Opening balance / Balance b/fwd	*		
	Closing balance / Balance c/fwd	*		

* Delete as appropriate

If you need more space, carry your balance forward to the next page.
If you have reached the end of your month/period, then check that the Closing balance
above, agrees to your Bank Statement for the same period.
Use a fresh page for each new month.

INCOME/EXPENSE LEDGER

Month:		Year:		

Date	Description	Income	Expense	Balance
	Opening balance / Balance b/fwd	*		
	Closing balance / Balance c/fwd	*		

* Delete as appropriate

If you need more space, carry your balance forward to the next page.
If you have reached the end of your month/period, then check that the Closing balance
above, agrees to your Bank Statement for the same period.
Use a fresh page for each new month.

INCOME/EXPENSE LEDGER

Month:			Year:	

Date	Description	Income	Expense	Balance
	Opening balance / Balance b/fwd	*		
	Closing balance / Balance c/fwd	*		

* Delete as appropriate

If you need more space, carry your balance forward to the next page.
If you have reached the end of your month/period, then check that the Closing balance
above, agrees to your Bank Statement for the same period.
Use a fresh page for each new month.

INCOME/EXPENSE LEDGER

Month:			Year:	

Date	Description	Income	Expense	Balance
	Opening balance / Balance b/fwd *			
	Closing balance / Balance c/fwd *			

* Delete as appropriate

If you need more space, carry your balance forward to the next page.
If you have reached the end of your month/period, then check that the Closing balance above, agrees to your Bank Statement for the same period.
Use a fresh page for each new month.

INCOME/EXPENSE LEDGER

Month:		Year:		

Date	Description	Income	Expense	Balance
	Opening balance / Balance b/fwd *			
	Closing balance / Balance c/fwd *			

* Delete as appropriate

If you need more space, carry your balance forward to the next page.
If you have reached the end of your month/period, then check that the Closing balance above, agrees to your Bank Statement for the same period.
Use a fresh page for each new month.

INCOME/EXPENSE LEDGER

Month:			Year:	

Date	Description	Income	Expense	Balance
	Opening balance / Balance b/fwd *			
	Closing balance / Balance c/fwd *			

* Delete as appropriate

If you need more space, carry your balance forward to the next page.
If you have reached the end of your month/period, then check that the Closing balance above, agrees to your Bank Statement for the same period.
Use a fresh page for each new month.

INCOME/EXPENSE LEDGER

Month:		Year:		

Date	Description	Income	Expense	Balance
	Opening balance / Balance b/fwd	*		
	Closing balance / Balance c/fwd	*		

* Delete as appropriate

If you need more space, carry your balance forward to the next page.
If you have reached the end of your month/period, then check that the Closing balance
above, agrees to your Bank Statement for the same period.
Use a fresh page for each new month.

INCOME/EXPENSE LEDGER

Month:			Year:	

Date	Description	Income	Expense	Balance
	Opening balance / Balance b/fwd	*		
	Closing balance / Balance c/fwd	*		

* Delete as appropriate

If you need more space, carry your balance forward to the next page.
If you have reached the end of your month/period, then check that the Closing balance
above, agrees to your Bank Statement for the same period.
Use a fresh page for each new month.

INCOME/EXPENSE LEDGER

Month:		Year:		
Date	Description	Income	Expense	Balance
	Opening balance / Balance b/fwd *			
	Closing balance / Balance c/fwd *			

* Delete as appropriate

If you need more space, carry your balance forward to the next page.
If you have reached the end of your month/period, then check that the Closing balance
above, agrees to your Bank Statement for the same period.
Use a fresh page for each new month.

INCOME/EXPENSE LEDGER

Month:			Year:	

Date	Description	Income	Expense	Balance
	Opening balance / Balance b/fwd	*		
	Closing balance / Balance c/fwd	*		

* Delete as appropriate

If you need more space, carry your balance forward to the next page.
If you have reached the end of your month/period, then check that the Closing balance
above, agrees to your Bank Statement for the same period.
Use a fresh page for each new month.

INCOME/EXPENSE LEDGER

Month:		Year:		

Date	Description	Income	Expense	Balance
	Opening balance / Balance b/fwd *			
	Closing balance / Balance c/fwd *			

* Delete as appropriate

If you need more space, carry your balance forward to the next page.
If you have reached the end of your month/period, then check that the Closing balance
above, agrees to your Bank Statement for the same period.
Use a fresh page for each new month.

INCOME/EXPENSE LEDGER

Month:	Year:

Date	Description	Income	Expense	Balance
	Opening balance / Balance b/fwd	*		
	Closing balance / Balance c/fwd	*		

* Delete as appropriate

If you need more space, carry your balance forward to the next page.
If you have reached the end of your month/period, then check that the Closing balance above, agrees to your Bank Statement for the same period.
Use a fresh page for each new month.

INCOME/EXPENSE LEDGER

Month:		Year:		

Date	Description	Income	Expense	Balance
	Opening balance / Balance b/fwd	*		
	Closing balance / Balance c/fwd	*		

* Delete as appropriate

If you need more space, carry your balance forward to the next page.
If you have reached the end of your month/period, then check that the Closing balance
above, agrees to your Bank Statement for the same period.
Use a fresh page for each new month.

INCOME/EXPENSE LEDGER

Month:				Year:

Date	Description	Income	Expense	Balance
	Opening balance / Balance b/fwd	*		
	Closing balance / Balance c/fwd	*		

* Delete as appropriate

If you need more space, carry your balance forward to the next page.
If you have reached the end of your month/period, then check that the Closing balance
above, agrees to your Bank Statement for the same period.
Use a fresh page for each new month.

INCOME/EXPENSE LEDGER

Month:		Year:		

Date	Description	Income	Expense	Balance
	Opening balance / Balance b/fwd *			
	Closing balance / Balance c/fwd *			

* Delete as appropriate

If you need more space, carry your balance forward to the next page.
If you have reached the end of your month/period, then check that the Closing balance above, agrees to your Bank Statement for the same period.
Use a fresh page for each new month.

INCOME/EXPENSE LEDGER

Month:			Year:		

Date	Description	Income	Expense	Balance
	Opening balance / Balance b/fwd	*		
	Closing balance / Balance c/fwd	*		

* Delete as appropriate

If you need more space, carry your balance forward to the next page.
If you have reached the end of your month/period, then check that the Closing balance above, agrees to your Bank Statement for the same period.
Use a fresh page for each new month.

INCOME/EXPENSE LEDGER

Month: **Year:**

Date	Description	Income	Expense	Balance
	Opening balance / Balance b/fwd *			
	Closing balance / Balance c/fwd *			

* Delete as appropriate

If you need more space, carry your balance forward to the next page.
If you have reached the end of your month/period, then check that the Closing balance above, agrees to your Bank Statement for the same period.
Use a fresh page for each new month.

INCOME/EXPENSE LEDGER

Month:	Year:

Date	Description	Income	Expense	Balance
	Opening balance / Balance b/fwd	*		
	Closing balance / Balance c/fwd	*		

* Delete as appropriate

If you need more space, carry your balance forward to the next page.
If you have reached the end of your month/period, then check that the Closing balance
above, agrees to your Bank Statement for the same period.
Use a fresh page for each new month.

INCOME/EXPENSE LEDGER

Month:		Year:		

Date	Description	Income	Expense	Balance
	Opening balance / Balance b/fwd	*		
	Closing balance / Balance c/fwd	*		

* Delete as appropriate

If you need more space, carry your balance forward to the next page.
If you have reached the end of your month/period, then check that the Closing balance above, agrees to your Bank Statement for the same period.
Use a fresh page for each new month.

INCOME/EXPENSE LEDGER

| Month: | | | | Year: |

Date	Description	Income	Expense	Balance
	Opening balance / Balance b/fwd *			
	Closing balance / Balance c/fwd *			

* Delete as appropriate

If you need more space, carry your balance forward to the next page.
If you have reached the end of your month/period, then check that the Closing balance
above, agrees to your Bank Statement for the same period.
Use a fresh page for each new month.

INCOME/EXPENSE LEDGER

Month: **Year:**

Date	Description	Income	Expense	Balance
	Opening balance / Balance b/fwd *			
	Closing balance / Balance c/fwd *			

* Delete as appropriate

If you need more space, carry your balance forward to the next page.
If you have reached the end of your month/period, then check that the Closing balance above, agrees to your Bank Statement for the same period.
Use a fresh page for each new month.

INCOME/EXPENSE LEDGER

Month:			Year:	

Date	Description	Income	Expense	Balance
	Opening balance / Balance b/fwd	*		
	Closing balance / Balance c/fwd	*		

* Delete as appropriate

If you need more space, carry your balance forward to the next page.
If you have reached the end of your month/period, then check that the Closing balance
above, agrees to your Bank Statement for the same period.
Use a fresh page for each new month.

INCOME/EXPENSE LEDGER

Month:		Year:		

Date	Description	Income	Expense	Balance
	Opening balance / Balance b/fwd *			
	Closing balance / Balance c/fwd *			

* Delete as appropriate

If you need more space, carry your balance forward to the next page.
If you have reached the end of your month/period, then check that the Closing balance above, agrees to your Bank Statement for the same period.
Use a fresh page for each new month.

INCOME/EXPENSE LEDGER

Month: _____

Year: _____

Date	Description	Income	Expense	Balance
	Opening balance / Balance b/fwd *			
	Closing balance / Balance c/fwd *			

* Delete as appropriate

If you need more space, carry your balance forward to the next page.
If you have reached the end of your month/period, then check that the Closing balance
above, agrees to your Bank Statement for the same period.
Use a fresh page for each new month.

INCOME/EXPENSE LEDGER

Month:			Year:	

Date	Description	Income	Expense	Balance
	Opening balance / Balance b/fwd	*		
	Closing balance / Balance c/fwd	*		

* Delete as appropriate

If you need more space, carry your balance forward to the next page.
If you have reached the end of your month/period, then check that the Closing balance above, agrees to your Bank Statement for the same period.
Use a fresh page for each new month.

INCOME/EXPENSE LEDGER

Month:	Year:

Date	Description	Income	Expense	Balance
	Opening balance / Balance b/fwd	*		
	Closing balance / Balance c/fwd	*		

* Delete as appropriate

If you need more space, carry your balance forward to the next page.
If you have reached the end of your month/period, then check that the Closing balance above, agrees to your Bank Statement for the same period.
Use a fresh page for each new month.

INCOME/EXPENSE LEDGER

Month:				Year:

Date	Description	Income	Expense	Balance
	Opening balance / Balance b/fwd	*		
	Closing balance / Balance c/fwd	*		

* Delete as appropriate

If you need more space, carry your balance forward to the next page.
If you have reached the end of your month/period, then check that the Closing balance above, agrees to your Bank Statement for the same period.
Use a fresh page for each new month.

INCOME/EXPENSE LEDGER

Month:		Year:		

Date	Description	Income	Expense	Balance
	Opening balance / Balance b/fwd	*		
	Closing balance / Balance c/fwd	*		

* Delete as appropriate

If you need more space, carry your balance forward to the next page.
If you have reached the end of your month/period, then check that the Closing balance above, agrees to your Bank Statement for the same period.
Use a fresh page for each new month.

INCOME/EXPENSE LEDGER

Month: | **Year:**

Date	Description	Income	Expense	Balance
	Opening balance / Balance b/fwd *			
	Closing balance / Balance c/fwd *			

* Delete as appropriate

If you need more space, carry your balance forward to the next page.
If you have reached the end of your month/period, then check that the Closing balance
above, agrees to your Bank Statement for the same period.
Use a fresh page for each new month.

INCOME/EXPENSE LEDGER

Month:			Year:	

Date	Description	Income	Expense	Balance
	Opening balance / Balance b/fwd *			
	Closing balance / Balance c/fwd *			

* Delete as appropriate

If you need more space, carry your balance forward to the next page.
If you have reached the end of your month/period, then check that the Closing balance above, agrees to your Bank Statement for the same period.
Use a fresh page for each new month.

INCOME/EXPENSE LEDGER

Month:			Year:	

Date	Description	Income	Expense	Balance
	Opening balance / Balance b/fwd	*		
	Closing balance / Balance c/fwd	*		

* Delete as appropriate

If you need more space, carry your balance forward to the next page.
If you have reached the end of your month/period, then check that the Closing balance
above, agrees to your Bank Statement for the same period.
Use a fresh page for each new month.

INCOME/EXPENSE LEDGER

Month:	Year:

Date	Description	Income	Expense	Balance
	Opening balance / Balance b/fwd *			
	Closing balance / Balance c/fwd *			

* Delete as appropriate

If you need more space, carry your balance forward to the next page.
If you have reached the end of your month/period, then check that the Closing balance
above, agrees to your Bank Statement for the same period.
Use a fresh page for each new month.

INCOME/EXPENSE LEDGER

Month:			Year:	

Date	Description	Income	Expense	Balance
	Opening balance / Balance b/fwd *			
	Closing balance / Balance c/fwd *			

* Delete as appropriate

If you need more space, carry your balance forward to the next page.
If you have reached the end of your month/period, then check that the Closing balance above, agrees to your Bank Statement for the same period.
Use a fresh page for each new month.

INCOME/EXPENSE LEDGER

Month:		Year:		

Date	Description	Income	Expense	Balance
	Opening balance / Balance b/fwd	*		
	Closing balance / Balance c/fwd	*		

* Delete as appropriate

If you need more space, carry your balance forward to the next page.
If you have reached the end of your month/period, then check that the Closing balance
above, agrees to your Bank Statement for the same period.
Use a fresh page for each new month.

INCOME/EXPENSE LEDGER

Month: **Year:**

Date	Description	Income	Expense	Balance
	Opening balance / Balance b/fwd *			
	Closing balance / Balance c/fwd *			

* Delete as appropriate

If you need more space, carry your balance forward to the next page.
If you have reached the end of your month/period, then check that the Closing balance above, agrees to your Bank Statement for the same period.
Use a fresh page for each new month.

INCOME/EXPENSE LEDGER

Month:		Year:		

Date	Description	Income	Expense	Balance
	Opening balance / Balance b/fwd *			
	Closing balance / Balance c/fwd *			

* Delete as appropriate

If you need more space, carry your balance forward to the next page.
If you have reached the end of your month/period, then check that the Closing balance
above, agrees to your Bank Statement for the same period.
Use a fresh page for each new month.

INCOME/EXPENSE LEDGER

Month: | **Year:**

Date	Description	Income	Expense	Balance
	Opening balance / Balance b/fwd	*		
	Closing balance / Balance c/fwd	*		

* Delete as appropriate

If you need more space, carry your balance forward to the next page.
If you have reached the end of your month/period, then check that the Closing balance
above, agrees to your Bank Statement for the same period.
Use a fresh page for each new month.

INCOME/EXPENSE LEDGER

Month: **Year:**

Date	Description	Income	Expense	Balance
	Opening balance / Balance b/fwd	*		
	Closing balance / Balance c/fwd	*		

* Delete as appropriate

If you need more space, carry your balance forward to the next page.
If you have reached the end of your month/period, then check that the Closing balance above, agrees to your Bank Statement for the same period.
Use a fresh page for each new month.

INCOME/EXPENSE LEDGER

Month:			Year:	

Date	Description	Income	Expense	Balance
	Opening balance / Balance b/fwd	*		
	Closing balance / Balance c/fwd	*		

* Delete as appropriate

If you need more space, carry your balance forward to the next page.
If you have reached the end of your month/period, then check that the Closing balance
above, agrees to your Bank Statement for the same period.
Use a fresh page for each new month.

INCOME/EXPENSE LEDGER

Month:			Year:	

Date	Description	Income	Expense	Balance
	Opening balance / Balance b/fwd	*		
	Closing balance / Balance c/fwd	*		

* Delete as appropriate

If you need more space, carry your balance forward to the next page.
If you have reached the end of your month/period, then check that the Closing balance
above, agrees to your Bank Statement for the same period.
Use a fresh page for each new month.

INCOME/EXPENSE LEDGER

Month:			Year:		

Date	Description	Income	Expense	Balance
	Opening balance / Balance b/fwd *			
	Closing balance / Balance c/fwd *			

* Delete as appropriate

If you need more space, carry your balance forward to the next page.
If you have reached the end of your month/period, then check that the Closing balance above, agrees to your Bank Statement for the same period.
Use a fresh page for each new month.

INCOME/EXPENSE LEDGER

Month:	Year:

Date	Description	Income	Expense	Balance
	Opening balance / Balance b/fwd *			
	Closing balance / Balance c/fwd *			

* Delete as appropriate

If you need more space, carry your balance forward to the next page.
If you have reached the end of your month/period, then check that the Closing balance
above, agrees to your Bank Statement for the same period.
Use a fresh page for each new month.

INCOME/EXPENSE LEDGER

Month: _____ **Year:** _____

Date	Description	Income	Expense	Balance
	Opening balance / Balance b/fwd	*		
	Closing balance / Balance c/fwd	*		

* Delete as appropriate

If you need more space, carry your balance forward to the next page.
If you have reached the end of your month/period, then check that the Closing balance above, agrees to your Bank Statement for the same period.
Use a fresh page for each new month.

INCOME/EXPENSE LEDGER

Month:			Year:	

Date	Description	Income	Expense	Balance
	Opening balance / Balance b/fwd *			
	Closing balance / Balance c/fwd *			

* Delete as appropriate

If you need more space, carry your balance forward to the next page.
If you have reached the end of your month/period, then check that the Closing balance above, agrees to your Bank Statement for the same period.
Use a fresh page for each new month.

INCOME/EXPENSE LEDGER

Month: **Year:**

Date	Description	Income	Expense	Balance
	Opening balance / Balance b/fwd	*		
	Closing balance / Balance c/fwd	*		

* Delete as appropriate

If you need more space, carry your balance forward to the next page.
If you have reached the end of your month/period, then check that the Closing balance above, agrees to your Bank Statement for the same period.
Use a fresh page for each new month.

INCOME/EXPENSE LEDGER

Month:			Year:		

Date	Description	Income	Expense	Balance
	Opening balance / Balance b/fwd	*		
	Closing balance / Balance c/fwd	*		

* Delete as appropriate

If you need more space, carry your balance forward to the next page.
If you have reached the end of your month/period, then check that the Closing balance above, agrees to your Bank Statement for the same period.
Use a fresh page for each new month.

INCOME/EXPENSE LEDGER

Month:			Year:	

Date	Description	Income	Expense	Balance
	Opening balance / Balance b/fwd *			
	Closing balance / Balance c/fwd *			

* Delete as appropriate

If you need more space, carry your balance forward to the next page.
If you have reached the end of your month/period, then check that the Closing balance
above, agrees to your Bank Statement for the same period.
Use a fresh page for each new month.

INCOME/EXPENSE LEDGER

Month:			Year:	

Date	Description	Income	Expense	Balance
	Opening balance / Balance b/fwd *			
	Closing balance / Balance c/fwd *			

* Delete as appropriate

If you need more space, carry your balance forward to the next page.
If you have reached the end of your month/period, then check that the Closing balance
above, agrees to your Bank Statement for the same period.
Use a fresh page for each new month.

INCOME/EXPENSE LEDGER

Month:		Year:		

Date	Description	Income	Expense	Balance
	Opening balance / Balance b/fwd	*		
	Closing balance / Balance c/fwd	*		

* Delete as appropriate

If you need more space, carry your balance forward to the next page.
If you have reached the end of your month/period, then check that the Closing balance
above, agrees to your Bank Statement for the same period.
Use a fresh page for each new month.

INCOME/EXPENSE LEDGER

| Month: | | Year: | | |

Date	Description	Income	Expense	Balance
	Opening balance / Balance b/fwd *			
	Closing balance / Balance c/fwd *			

* Delete as appropriate

If you need more space, carry your balance forward to the next page.
If you have reached the end of your month/period, then check that the Closing balance above, agrees to your Bank Statement for the same period.
Use a fresh page for each new month.

INCOME/EXPENSE LEDGER

Month:				

Year:				

Date	Description	Income	Expense	Balance
	Opening balance / Balance b/fwd	*		
	Closing balance / Balance c/fwd	*		

* Delete as appropriate

If you need more space, carry your balance forward to the next page.
If you have reached the end of your month/period, then check that the Closing balance
above, agrees to your Bank Statement for the same period.
Use a fresh page for each new month.

INCOME/EXPENSE LEDGER

Month:			Year:	

Date	Description	Income	Expense	Balance
	Opening balance / Balance b/fwd	*		
	Closing balance / Balance c/fwd	*		

* Delete as appropriate

If you need more space, carry your balance forward to the next page.
If you have reached the end of your month/period, then check that the Closing balance above, agrees to your Bank Statement for the same period.
Use a fresh page for each new month.

INCOME/EXPENSE LEDGER

Month:

Year:

Date	Description	Income	Expense	Balance
	Opening balance / Balance b/fwd *			
	Closing balance / Balance c/fwd *			

* Delete as appropriate

If you need more space, carry your balance forward to the next page.
If you have reached the end of your month/period, then check that the Closing balance
above, agrees to your Bank Statement for the same period.
Use a fresh page for each new month.

INCOME/EXPENSE LEDGER

Month:		Year:		

Date	Description	Income	Expense	Balance
	Opening balance / Balance b/fwd *			
	Closing balance / Balance c/fwd *			

* Delete as appropriate

If you need more space, carry your balance forward to the next page.
If you have reached the end of your month/period, then check that the Closing balance above, agrees to your Bank Statement for the same period.
Use a fresh page for each new month.

INCOME/EXPENSE LEDGER

Month:					

Year:					

Date	Description	Income	Expense	Balance
	Opening balance / Balance b/fwd	*		
	Closing balance / Balance c/fwd	*		

* Delete as appropriate

If you need more space, carry your balance forward to the next page.
If you have reached the end of your month/period, then check that the Closing balance
above, agrees to your Bank Statement for the same period.
Use a fresh page for each new month.

INCOME/EXPENSE LEDGER

Month:			Year:	

Date	Description	Income	Expense	Balance
	Opening balance / Balance b/fwd *			
	Closing balance / Balance c/fwd *			

* Delete as appropriate

If you need more space, carry your balance forward to the next page.
If you have reached the end of your month/period, then check that the Closing balance
above, agrees to your Bank Statement for the same period.
Use a fresh page for each new month.

INCOME/EXPENSE LEDGER

Month:		Year:		

Date	Description	Income	Expense	Balance
	Opening balance / Balance b/fwd	*		
	Closing balance / Balance c/fwd	*		

* Delete as appropriate

If you need more space, carry your balance forward to the next page.
If you have reached the end of your month/period, then check that the Closing balance above, agrees to your Bank Statement for the same period.
Use a fresh page for each new month.

INCOME/EXPENSE LEDGER

Month:		Year:		

Date	Description	Income	Expense	Balance
	Opening balance / Balance b/fwd	*		
	Closing balance / Balance c/fwd	*		

* Delete as appropriate

If you need more space, carry your balance forward to the next page.
If you have reached the end of your month/period, then check that the Closing balance above, agrees to your Bank Statement for the same period.
Use a fresh page for each new month.

INCOME/EXPENSE LEDGER

Month:		Year:		

Date	Description	Income	Expense	Balance
	Opening balance / Balance b/fwd	*		
	Closing balance / Balance c/fwd	*		

* Delete as appropriate

If you need more space, carry your balance forward to the next page.
If you have reached the end of your month/period, then check that the Closing balance above, agrees to your Bank Statement for the same period.
Use a fresh page for each new month.

INCOME/EXPENSE LEDGER

Month:			Year:	

Date	Description	Income	Expense	Balance
	Opening balance / Balance b/fwd *			
	Closing balance / Balance c/fwd *			

* Delete as appropriate

If you need more space, carry your balance forward to the next page.
If you have reached the end of your month/period, then check that the Closing balance above, agrees to your Bank Statement for the same period.
Use a fresh page for each new month.

INCOME/EXPENSE LEDGER

Month:

Year:

Date	Description	Income	Expense	Balance
	Opening balance / Balance b/fwd	*		
	Closing balance / Balance c/fwd	*		

* Delete as appropriate

If you need more space, carry your balance forward to the next page.
If you have reached the end of your month/period, then check that the Closing balance
above, agrees to your Bank Statement for the same period.
Use a fresh page for each new month.

INCOME/EXPENSE LEDGER

Month:	Year:

Date	Description	Income	Expense	Balance
	Opening balance / Balance b/fwd	*		
	Closing balance / Balance c/fwd	*		

* Delete as appropriate

If you need more space, carry your balance forward to the next page.
If you have reached the end of your month/period, then check that the Closing balance
above, agrees to your Bank Statement for the same period.
Use a fresh page for each new month.

INCOME/EXPENSE LEDGER

Month:	Year:

Date	Description	Income	Expense	Balance
	Opening balance / Balance b/fwd *			
	Closing balance / Balance c/fwd *			

* Delete as appropriate

If you need more space, carry your balance forward to the next page.
If you have reached the end of your month/period, then check that the Closing balance
above, agrees to your Bank Statement for the same period.
Use a fresh page for each new month.

INCOME/EXPENSE LEDGER

Month:			Year:	

Date	Description	Income	Expense	Balance
	Opening balance / Balance b/fwd *			
	Closing balance / Balance c/fwd *			

* Delete as appropriate

If you need more space, carry your balance forward to the next page.
If you have reached the end of your month/period, then check that the Closing balance
above, agrees to your Bank Statement for the same period.
Use a fresh page for each new month.

INCOME/EXPENSE LEDGER

Month:		Year:		

Date	Description	Income	Expense	Balance
	Opening balance / Balance b/fwd *			
	Closing balance / Balance c/fwd *			

* Delete as appropriate

If you need more space, carry your balance forward to the next page.
If you have reached the end of your month/period, then check that the Closing balance
above, agrees to your Bank Statement for the same period.
Use a fresh page for each new month.

INCOME/EXPENSE LEDGER

Month:		Year:		

Date	Description	Income	Expense	Balance
	Opening balance / Balance b/fwd *			
	Closing balance / Balance c/fwd *			

* Delete as appropriate

If you need more space, carry your balance forward to the next page.
If you have reached the end of your month/period, then check that the Closing balance above, agrees to your Bank Statement for the same period.
Use a fresh page for each new month.

INCOME/EXPENSE LEDGER

Month:			Year:	

Date	Description	Income	Expense	Balance
	Opening balance / Balance b/fwd	*		
	Closing balance / Balance c/fwd	*		

* Delete as appropriate

If you need more space, carry your balance forward to the next page.
If you have reached the end of your month/period, then check that the Closing balance
above, agrees to your Bank Statement for the same period.
Use a fresh page for each new month.

INCOME/EXPENSE LEDGER

Month:			Year:	

Date	Description	Income	Expense	Balance
	Opening balance / Balance b/fwd *			
	Closing balance / Balance c/fwd *			

* Delete as appropriate

If you need more space, carry your balance forward to the next page.
If you have reached the end of your month/period, then check that the Closing balance
above, agrees to your Bank Statement for the same period.
Use a fresh page for each new month.

INCOME/EXPENSE LEDGER

Month:			Year:		

Date	Description	Income	Expense	Balance
	Opening balance / Balance b/fwd *			
	Closing balance / Balance c/fwd *			

* Delete as appropriate

If you need more space, carry your balance forward to the next page.
If you have reached the end of your month/period, then check that the Closing balance
above, agrees to your Bank Statement for the same period.
Use a fresh page for each new month.

INCOME/EXPENSE LEDGER

Month:		Year:		

Date	Description	Income	Expense	Balance
	Opening balance / Balance b/fwd *			
	Closing balance / Balance c/fwd *			

* Delete as appropriate

If you need more space, carry your balance forward to the next page.
If you have reached the end of your month/period, then check that the Closing balance above, agrees to your Bank Statement for the same period.
Use a fresh page for each new month.

INCOME/EXPENSE LEDGER

Month:		Year:		

Date	Description	Income	Expense	Balance
	Opening balance / Balance b/fwd *			
	Closing balance / Balance c/fwd *			

* Delete as appropriate

If you need more space, carry your balance forward to the next page.
If you have reached the end of your month/period, then check that the Closing balance
above, agrees to your Bank Statement for the same period.
Use a fresh page for each new month.

INCOME/EXPENSE LEDGER

Month:			Year:	

Date	Description	Income	Expense	Balance
	Opening balance / Balance b/fwd *			
	Closing balance / Balance c/fwd *			

* Delete as appropriate

If you need more space, carry your balance forward to the next page.
If you have reached the end of your month/period, then check that the Closing balance above, agrees to your Bank Statement for the same period.
Use a fresh page for each new month.

INCOME/EXPENSE LEDGER

Month:		Year:		

Date	Description	Income	Expense	Balance
	Opening balance / Balance b/fwd	*		
	Closing balance / Balance c/fwd	*		

* Delete as appropriate

If you need more space, carry your balance forward to the next page.
If you have reached the end of your month/period, then check that the Closing balance
above, agrees to your Bank Statement for the same period.
Use a fresh page for each new month.

INCOME/EXPENSE LEDGER

Month:			Year:		

Date	Description	Income	Expense	Balance
	Opening balance / Balance b/fwd *			
	Closing balance / Balance c/fwd *			

* Delete as appropriate

If you need more space, carry your balance forward to the next page.
If you have reached the end of your month/period, then check that the Closing balance
above, agrees to your Bank Statement for the same period.
Use a fresh page for each new month.

INCOME/EXPENSE LEDGER

Month:		Year:		

Date	Description	Income	Expense	Balance
	Opening balance / Balance b/fwd *			
	Closing balance / Balance c/fwd *			

* Delete as appropriate

If you need more space, carry your balance forward to the next page.
If you have reached the end of your month/period, then check that the Closing balance
above, agrees to your Bank Statement for the same period.
Use a fresh page for each new month.

INCOME/EXPENSE LEDGER

Month:			Year:	

Date	Description	Income	Expense	Balance
	Opening balance / Balance b/fwd *			
	Closing balance / Balance c/fwd *			

* Delete as appropriate

If you need more space, carry your balance forward to the next page.
If you have reached the end of your month/period, then check that the Closing balance
above, agrees to your Bank Statement for the same period.
Use a fresh page for each new month.

INCOME/EXPENSE LEDGER

Month:		Year:		

Date	Description	Income	Expense	Balance
	Opening balance / Balance b/fwd	*		
	Closing balance / Balance c/fwd	*		

* Delete as appropriate

If you need more space, carry your balance forward to the next page.
If you have reached the end of your month/period, then check that the Closing balance
above, agrees to your Bank Statement for the same period.
Use a fresh page for each new month.

INCOME/EXPENSE LEDGER

| Month: | | | Year: | |

Date	Description	Income	Expense	Balance
	Opening balance / Balance b/fwd *			
	Closing balance / Balance c/fwd *			

* Delete as appropriate

If you need more space, carry your balance forward to the next page.
If you have reached the end of your month/period, then check that the Closing balance
above, agrees to your Bank Statement for the same period.
Use a fresh page for each new month.

INCOME/EXPENSE LEDGER

Month: **Year:**

Date	Description	Income	Expense	Balance
	Opening balance / Balance b/fwd	*		
	Closing balance / Balance c/fwd	*		

* Delete as appropriate

If you need more space, carry your balance forward to the next page.
If you have reached the end of your month/period, then check that the Closing balance
above, agrees to your Bank Statement for the same period.
Use a fresh page for each new month.

INCOME/EXPENSE LEDGER

Month:			Year:	

Date	Description	Income	Expense	Balance
	Opening balance / Balance b/fwd	*		
	Closing balance / Balance c/fwd	*		

* Delete as appropriate

If you need more space, carry your balance forward to the next page.
If you have reached the end of your month/period, then check that the Closing balance
above, agrees to your Bank Statement for the same period.
Use a fresh page for each new month.

INCOME/EXPENSE LEDGER

Month:			Year:		

Date	Description	Income	Expense	Balance
	Opening balance / Balance b/fwd	*		
	Closing balance / Balance c/fwd	*		

* Delete as appropriate

If you need more space, carry your balance forward to the next page.
If you have reached the end of your month/period, then check that the Closing balance
above, agrees to your Bank Statement for the same period.
Use a fresh page for each new month.

INCOME/EXPENSE LEDGER

Month:	Year:

Date	Description	Income	Expense	Balance
	Opening balance / Balance b/fwd	*		
	Closing balance / Balance c/fwd	*		

* Delete as appropriate

If you need more space, carry your balance forward to the next page.
If you have reached the end of your month/period, then check that the Closing balance
above, agrees to your Bank Statement for the same period.
Use a fresh page for each new month.

INCOME/EXPENSE LEDGER

Month:	Year:

Date	Description	Income	Expense	Balance
	Opening balance / Balance b/fwd	*		
	Closing balance / Balance c/fwd	*		

* Delete as appropriate

If you need more space, carry your balance forward to the next page.
If you have reached the end of your month/period, then check that the Closing balance
above, agrees to your Bank Statement for the same period.
Use a fresh page for each new month.

INCOME/EXPENSE LEDGER

Month:			Year:		

Date	Description	Income	Expense	Balance
	Opening balance / Balance b/fwd	*		
	Closing balance / Balance c/fwd	*		

* Delete as appropriate

If you need more space, carry your balance forward to the next page.
If you have reached the end of your month/period, then check that the Closing balance above, agrees to your Bank Statement for the same period.
Use a fresh page for each new month.

INCOME/EXPENSE LEDGER

Month: | **Year:**

Date	Description	Income	Expense	Balance
	Opening balance / Balance b/fwd	*		
	Closing balance / Balance c/fwd	*		

* Delete as appropriate

If you need more space, carry your balance forward to the next page.
If you have reached the end of your month/period, then check that the Closing balance
above, agrees to your Bank Statement for the same period.
Use a fresh page for each new month.

INCOME/EXPENSE LEDGER

Month:	Year:

Date	Description	Income	Expense	Balance
	Opening balance / Balance b/fwd	*		
	Closing balance / Balance c/fwd	*		

* Delete as appropriate

If you need more space, carry your balance forward to the next page.
If you have reached the end of your month/period, then check that the Closing balance
above, agrees to your Bank Statement for the same period.
Use a fresh page for each new month.

INCOME/EXPENSE LEDGER

Month:	Year:

Date	Description	Income	Expense	Balance
	Opening balance / Balance b/fwd *			
	Closing balance / Balance c/fwd *			

* Delete as appropriate

If you need more space, carry your balance forward to the next page.
If you have reached the end of your month/period, then check that the Closing balance above, agrees to your Bank Statement for the same period.
Use a fresh page for each new month.

INCOME/EXPENSE LEDGER

Month:			Year:	

Date	Description	Income	Expense	Balance
	Opening balance / Balance b/fwd	*		
	Closing balance / Balance c/fwd	*		

* Delete as appropriate

If you need more space, carry your balance forward to the next page.
If you have reached the end of your month/period, then check that the Closing balance
above, agrees to your Bank Statement for the same period.
Use a fresh page for each new month.

INCOME/EXPENSE LEDGER

Month:	Year:

Date	Description	Income	Expense	Balance
	Opening balance / Balance b/fwd	*		
	Closing balance / Balance c/fwd	*		

* Delete as appropriate

If you need more space, carry your balance forward to the next page.
If you have reached the end of your month/period, then check that the Closing balance
above, agrees to your Bank Statement for the same period.
Use a fresh page for each new month.

INCOME/EXPENSE LEDGER

Month:	Year:

Date	Description	Income	Expense	Balance
	Opening balance / Balance b/fwd *			
	Closing balance / Balance c/fwd *			

> * Delete as appropriate

> If you need more space, carry your balance forward to the next page.
> If you have reached the end of your month/period, then check that the Closing balance
> above, agrees to your Bank Statement for the same period.
> Use a fresh page for each new month.

INCOME/EXPENSE LEDGER

Month: **Year:**

Date	Description	Income	Expense	Balance
	Opening balance / Balance b/fwd	*		
	Closing balance / Balance c/fwd	*		

* Delete as appropriate

If you need more space, carry your balance forward to the next page.
If you have reached the end of your month/period, then check that the Closing balance
above, agrees to your Bank Statement for the same period.
Use a fresh page for each new month.

INCOME/EXPENSE LEDGER

Month:		Year:		

Date	Description	Income	Expense	Balance
	Opening balance / Balance b/fwd	*		
	Closing balance / Balance c/fwd	*		

* Delete as appropriate

If you need more space, carry your balance forward to the next page.
If you have reached the end of your month/period, then check that the Closing balance
above, agrees to your Bank Statement for the same period.
Use a fresh page for each new month.

INCOME/EXPENSE LEDGER

Month:

Year:

Date	Description	Income	Expense	Balance
	Opening balance / Balance b/fwd	*		
	Closing balance / Balance c/fwd	*		

* Delete as appropriate

If you need more space, carry your balance forward to the next page.
If you have reached the end of your month/period, then check that the Closing balance
above, agrees to your Bank Statement for the same period.
Use a fresh page for each new month.

INCOME/EXPENSE LEDGER

Month:	Year:

Date	Description	Income	Expense	Balance
	Opening balance / Balance b/fwd	*		
	Closing balance / Balance c/fwd	*		

* Delete as appropriate

If you need more space, carry your balance forward to the next page.
If you have reached the end of your month/period, then check that the Closing balance above, agrees to your Bank Statement for the same period.
Use a fresh page for each new month.

INCOME/EXPENSE LEDGER

Month:

Year:

Date	Description	Income	Expense	Balance
	Opening balance / Balance b/fwd	*		
	Closing balance / Balance c/fwd	*		

* Delete as appropriate

If you need more space, carry your balance forward to the next page.
If you have reached the end of your month/period, then check that the Closing balance
above, agrees to your Bank Statement for the same period.
Use a fresh page for each new month.

INCOME/EXPENSE LEDGER

Month:		Year:		

Date	Description	Income	Expense	Balance
	Opening balance / Balance b/fwd *			
	Closing balance / Balance c/fwd *			

* Delete as appropriate

If you need more space, carry your balance forward to the next page.
If you have reached the end of your month/period, then check that the Closing balance above, agrees to your Bank Statement for the same period.
Use a fresh page for each new month.

INCOME/EXPENSE LEDGER

Month: **Year:**

Date	Description	Income	Expense	Balance
	Opening balance / Balance b/fwd	*		
	Closing balance / Balance c/fwd	*		

* Delete as appropriate

If you need more space, carry your balance forward to the next page.
If you have reached the end of your month/period, then check that the Closing balance
above, agrees to your Bank Statement for the same period.
Use a fresh page for each new month.

INCOME/EXPENSE LEDGER

Month:			Year:	

Date	Description	Income	Expense	Balance
	Opening balance / Balance b/fwd *			
	Closing balance / Balance c/fwd *			

* Delete as appropriate

If you need more space, carry your balance forward to the next page.
If you have reached the end of your month/period, then check that the Closing balance
above, agrees to your Bank Statement for the same period.
Use a fresh page for each new month.

INCOME/EXPENSE LEDGER

| Month: | | | Year: | |

Date	Description	Income	Expense	Balance
	Opening balance / Balance b/fwd *			
	Closing balance / Balance c/fwd *			

* Delete as appropriate

If you need more space, carry your balance forward to the next page.
If you have reached the end of your month/period, then check that the Closing balance
above, agrees to your Bank Statement for the same period.
Use a fresh page for each new month.

INCOME/EXPENSE LEDGER

Month: **Year:**

Date	Description	Income	Expense	Balance
	Opening balance / Balance b/fwd	*		
	Closing balance / Balance c/fwd	*		

* Delete as appropriate

If you need more space, carry your balance forward to the next page.
If you have reached the end of your month/period, then check that the Closing balance above, agrees to your Bank Statement for the same period.
Use a fresh page for each new month.

INCOME/EXPENSE LEDGER

Month:

Year:

Date	Description	Income	Expense	Balance
	Opening balance / Balance b/fwd	*		
	Closing balance / Balance c/fwd	*		

* Delete as appropriate

If you need more space, carry your balance forward to the next page.
If you have reached the end of your month/period, then check that the Closing balance above, agrees to your Bank Statement for the same period.
Use a fresh page for each new month.

INCOME/EXPENSE LEDGER

Month:			Year:	

Date	Description	Income	Expense	Balance
	Opening balance / Balance b/fwd *			
	Closing balance / Balance c/fwd *			

* Delete as appropriate

If you need more space, carry your balance forward to the next page.
If you have reached the end of your month/period, then check that the Closing balance
above, agrees to your Bank Statement for the same period.
Use a fresh page for each new month.

INCOME/EXPENSE LEDGER

Month:		Year:		

Date	Description	Income	Expense	Balance
	Opening balance / Balance b/fwd	*		
	Closing balance / Balance c/fwd	*		

* Delete as appropriate

If you need more space, carry your balance forward to the next page.
If you have reached the end of your month/period, then check that the Closing balance
above, agrees to your Bank Statement for the same period.
Use a fresh page for each new month.

INCOME/EXPENSE LEDGER

Month:	Year:

Date	Description	Income	Expense	Balance
	Opening balance / Balance b/fwd	*		
	Closing balance / Balance c/fwd	*		

* Delete as appropriate

If you need more space, carry your balance forward to the next page.
If you have reached the end of your month/period, then check that the Closing balance above, agrees to your Bank Statement for the same period.
Use a fresh page for each new month.

Printed in Great Britain
by Amazon

34418260R00069